A JOURNEY HOME

The humanitarian challenge in Kosovo

A JOURNEY HOME

The humanitarian challenge in Kosovo

United Nations High Commissioner for Refugees

This book is dedicated to David Riley, a man of remarkable stature, who displayed out-standing devotion to humanitarian causes. As UNHCR Chief of Mission in Kosovo from July 1999 to January 2000, he played a key role in assisting Kosovo refugees to return to their homes and survive the first winter after the 1999 crisis. David Riley passed away in Prishtinë / Priština on January 20, 2000. He is dearly missed by his friends and colleagues around the world.

This book is also dedicated to all the people of Kosovo for their work towards a brighter future and to all the aid workers for their commitment to humanitarian assistance.

ISBN 92-1-101031- 4

Editor in chief: Hélène Caux
Editors: Elizabeth Gaffney, Anna Greene, Ron Redmond

Photographers: Kael Alford, Hélène Caux, Radhika Chalasani, Barron Rachman, Hazir Reka, Andrew Testa
Contributing authors: Paula Ghedini, Dennis McNamara, Grainne O'Hara
Contributing editors: Kiran Kaur, Monica Llamazares, Rachel Wareham
Graphic designer: Srdjan Spasić
Cartographers: Merkur Beqiri, Argjent Nela

Funding for this project was provided by UNHCR and the Norwegian Royal Ministry of Foreign Affairs.

The photographs appearing in this book have been used with the permission of the holders of the rights thereof.
Photographic copyright by the individual photographer.
Text copyright by the individual author.
The maps were produced by the Humanitarian Community Information Center in Kosovo with UNHCR Geographic Information System Unit.

Unless otherwise stated, the book does not refer to events occurring after November 30, 2001.
The opinions expressed in this volume are those of the authors and do not necessarily represent official views of UNHCR. Unless otherwise stated, figures were provided by UNHCR.

Any queries can be addressed to:
hqfr00@unhcr.ch
helenecaux@yahoo.com

For more information on the work of UNHCR: www.unhcr.ch
UNHCR
CH-1211 Geneva 2
Switzerland

Contents

Acknowledgements

The editor thanks all those who contributed to the preparation of this book, in particular for their editorial assistance and constant support: Nana Anto-Awakyue, Esmé Epstein, Alexandra Geneste, Michael Kingsley-Nyinah, Lennart Kotsalainen, Veton Orana, Francoise Peyroux, Susan Reynolds, Mercedes Rose, Milčo Serafitmovski, Michèle Shapiro, and Astrid Van Genderen Stort.

Special gratitude goes to UNHCR staff member Kiran Kaur and to the staff of the British Military Hospital in Kosovo, in particular to Dr. Barry Price, for their crucial assistance in March 2001.

Special thanks to the local and international staff of all UNHCR offices in Kosovo for their understanding and their interest in this project, to the fearless UNHCR drivers for their patience, to UNHCR staff in Skopje for their support, and to the UNHCR Division of Information in Geneva for their advice.

UNHCR wishes to thank the Norwegian Royal Ministry of Foreign Affairs for its generous financial contribution to the publication of this volume.

Terminology

Kosovars refers to all the people of Kosovo regardless of ethnicity.
Albanians refers to Kosovo Albanians unless otherwise stated.
Serbs refers to Kosovo Serbs unless otherwise stated.
Roma, *Ashkaelia* and *Egyptians* refer to the Kosovo communities of Roma, Ashkaelia and Egyptians.

Refugee: In the 1951 UN Convention relating to the Status of Refugees, a refugee is defined as a person who "owing to a well-founded fear of being persecuted for reasons of race, religion, nationality, membership of a particular social group, or political opinion, is outside the country of his / her nationality, and unable to or, owing to such fear, is unwilling to avail himself / herself of the protection of that country …" In this volume, the word "refugee" is applied more widely; on occasions, it is used to refer to Kosovars in Kosovo who are in the process of exodus or return.

The English standard spelling Kosovo is used throughout the book. Its use does not imply any statement or particular viewpoint by UNHCR. In other texts, the reader might find the spelling "Kosova" which is the standard Albanian rendition, whereas the official Serbian is rendered "Kosovo and Metohija" / "Kosmet".
Serbia refers to the entity that, in this context, does not include Kosovo.
In this publication, FYR Macedonia is used to refer to the former Yugoslav Republic of Macedonia.

According to official UNMIK policy, the names of cities and villages are spelled in the forms used in both the Albanian and the Serbian languages. In this book, Albanian is used first, followed by Serbian, if the picture features Albanian-speaking people whereas Serbian is used first, followed by Albanian, if the picture features Serbian-speaking people.

The population of Kosovo currently comprises of about two million inhabitants from many different ethnic backgrounds. Approximately ninety per cent of the total population is Albanian by ethnicity, while Serbs represent the second largest group. The other main ethnic populations of Kosovo are Rom peoples (who divide themselves in three different groups: Roma, Ashkaelia and Egyptians), Croats, Turks, and Bosniaks. There are also other less numerous indigenous ethnic groups, including Gorani, Torbeshi, and Cherkezi.

Foreword

This book visually documents the consequences of one of the most traumatic events that has occurred in Europe at the end of the twentieth century – the war in Kosovo. The time period covered represents the high point of UNHCR's involvement for the people of Kosovo. The agency had been present in Prishtinë / Priština since 1992, but its work took on a greater significance after 1998, when the first mass expulsions of people from central rural areas resulted in an urgent need for emergency food and shelter. Some displaced persons were taken in by families in cities, others could only find safety living in the woods, under makeshift shelter. In 1999, as the situation deteriorated, over 850,000 people were forced from their homes to FYR Macedonia, Albania and Montenegro. They were assisted by the host governments and local communities, as well as by UNHCR, other UN agencies, international and local NGOs. It is from this point that the photographs in this volume start to document their story, beginning at the time Kosovo Albanians were forced into exile in neighbouring countries and further abroad.

Of course, many different types of violence had occurred before this time, particularly to the Albanians, a population that had suffered for many years under a repressive system. Two images of the violence that preceded the exodus are presented after this foreword as a basic visual context of the rapidly deteriorating situation in Kosovo before the NATO-led campaign. But for more extensive photo documentation of this period and the war itself, the reader is directed to other photojournalistic works. Whilst the images in this book illustrate the context of UNHCR's and other agencies' work during and after the war, attention has been given to ensure that this collection focuses on the people to whom the events happened, the kinds of help they received and the contributions they made, instead of specifically documenting the work of UNHCR.

The images show a cycle of refugee experience: from expulsion and flight, to life outside of Kosovo in camps or with host families, and the return home. They also show the domino-like effect of violence, as later other ethnic groups fled in anticipation of or in response to revenge attacks, or were confined in enclaves. The cycle closes by depicting some individuals or groups who are working to create a future where ethnic diversity is respected.

Although all these events took place recently, they are already becoming dim - overshadowed by different wars and new refugee movements, as well as by an increasingly intolerant worldwide political discourse that regards refugees and immigrants as nuisances whose rights need not be guaranteed. It is hoped that these photographs will serve as a reminder not only of the tragic events that took place in Kosovo, but also of the dignity and the essential humanity of the refugee.

A girl runs through the ruins of her home in Polac i Ri / Novo Poljance in the heart of Kosovo's Drenica region. The village was first shelled in 1998. Further destruction of houses by Yugoslav forces continued, including during the three months of the NATO bombing campaign. February 1999. *Photo by Andrew Testa*

An Albanian man takes his grandson back to the village of Llapushnik / Lapušnik after the withdrawal of Yugoslav forces who had been shelling the area. The family had to flee their home eight times between February 1998 and February 1999 because of repeated military attacks. February 1999. *Photo by Andrew Testa*

Introduction

By Dennis McNamara

Sporadic gunfire rattled in the distance as our small aid convoy rolled into the seemingly deserted central Kosovo town of Gllogoc / Glogovac on the morning of June 14, 1999. It was one day after the United Nations had returned to war-ravaged Kosovo, and the UN agencies were mounting their first relief operation since withdrawing nearly three months earlier at the start of the NATO bombing campaign.

NATO forces had not yet arrived in Gllogoc / Glogovac and the outskirts of the town were swarming with Yugoslav troops and militiamen assembling for their withdrawal from Kosovo. They glared at us from atop armoured vehicles as our trucks, carrying tons of flour and other aid supplies, pulled to a stop in an otherwise empty street. Where, we wondered nervously, were all of the civilians?

After several minutes, a few children emerged from the surrounding buildings, and timidly approached our small convoy despite the presence of a Yugoslav armoured vehicle on a nearby street-corner. Quickly, word of our arrival spread through the neighbourhood and hundreds of people began streaming into the streets. Overjoyed by our arrival, women and children gathered wildflowers from the surrounding fields and threw them to us as gifts of welcome. Pale and gaunt, many had not ventured outside for weeks. For the people of Gllogoc / Glogovac, the long nightmare - and the world's first "humanitarian war" - was over.

For UNHCR and the other humanitarian agencies, however, the battle was far from finished. In the chronology of major twentieth-century refugee emergencies, and in UNHCR's entire fifty-year history, the Kosovo crisis had one of the shortest turnaround-periods from the initial outflow of people to their eventual return. Within eleven weeks of the start of the NATO bombing campaign on March 24, 1999, nearly one million people fled or, in scenes hauntingly reminiscent of World War II Europe, were deported by train to neighbouring countries. A few months later, nearly all of them had returned home.

Initially, host governments, UNHCR and its humanitarian partners were overwhelmed by the magnitude and speed of the refugee exodus. Despite subsequent claims to the contrary, no one predicted or was prepared for such huge numbers of displaced persons. Just days before the exodus began, key governments were still trying to ensure peace could be achieved, urging preparations for the early implementation of the Rambouillet accords.

In Albania and the former Yugoslav Republic of Macedonia in particular, there were serious problems in providing adequate assistance and protection. These included securing admission for refugees into ethnically-sensitive FYR Macedonia; the challenges of rapidly setting up camps for hundreds of thousands of people in both Albania and FYR Macedonia; and coping with the looming security problems in Montenegro.

With the withdrawal of the Yugoslav army and paramilitaries from Kosovo in mid-June, the refugees began flooding home as quickly as they had fled. They joined hundreds of thousands who had remained inside the province, hiding in homes and apartments or wandering from village to village in search of food, shelter and safety. All over Kosovo, roads were jammed with people in cars, taxis, trucks, tractors, horse carts, and even wheelbarrows piled high with household belongings. Up to half a million people came home in three weeks. Within three months, nearly everyone had returned.

With NATO's entry, more than 300 aid agencies rushed into Kosovo to provide humanitarian assistance. Donors, satisfied that a major objective of the war had been achieved, put hundreds of millions of dollars into the aid effort. The

United Nations struggled, with some success, to provide a degree of co-ordination to the efforts of this disparate and variable group of humanitarians. In an area half the size of Switzerland, with just over two million inhabitants, this was to become, per capita, one of the largest relief programmes ever undertaken. Indeed, the huge response raised some disquieting questions about the disparities between Kosovo and other less high-profile areas in need, particularly in Africa.

Despite some predictions of freezing and starvation during that first difficult winter home, the resilient and determined Kosovars survived, thanks in part to the international aid effort that provided thousands of tons of emergency shelter materials, food and other assistance. But as the Kosovo Albanians rebuilt their lives, others living in the province saw theirs disintegrate. Serbs, Roma and some members of other minority groups, fearful of revenge attacks, began leaving in their own exodus. Within weeks of the arrival of the United Nations and NATO, over 150,000 had fled Kosovo, and more were to follow. Those remaining faced the possibility of harassment, intimidation and physical violence by some members of the Kosovo Albanian majority – who sometimes employed the same shameful tactics once used against them.

Today, the Albanian population of Gllogoc / Glogovac is no longer afraid to walk the streets of their own town. They, like others all over Kosovo, with the help of local and international organisations, have found ways to overcome their trauma, and to rebuild their homes and lives. And yet the cycles of Kosovo's violence continue, and there appears to be no guarantee of a happy ending – including for the hundreds of thousands of people who are still unable to return home, for the thousands who lost loved ones, for those whose family members are still missing or imprisoned in Serbia, or for those who continue to live in constant fear of possible revenge attacks.

This book provides a visual record of the terror and the continuing tragedy of Kosovo and its people, as well as their achievements. All of the people pictured on these pages – whatever their background or ethnic group – share something in common: all have suffered enormously.

Dennis McNamara, a twenty-five year long veteran of UNHCR operations worldwide, was Deputy Special Representative of the UN Secretary-General for Humanitarian Affairs in Kosovo and UNHCR Special Envoy for the Balkans from mid-1999 to mid-2000.

EXODUS

Exodus

By Paula Ghedini

Dusk was falling and the air was thick with smoke from thousands of small fires stoked for warmth or for cooking an evening meal. Dazed and exhausted, two UNHCR colleagues and I trudged through the muddy fields of Blace. It was just a few days after the beginning of the NATO bombing campaign and we were trying to determine how to assist the many tens of thousands of refugees who had converged on this hellish patch of borderland between Kosovo and FYR Macedonia.

Muffled sobs rose above the din and the stench of the makeshift refugee site. I thought I heard my name being called, but put it down to a trick of my overwhelmed mind when suddenly I was embraced from behind. It was Blerta, a friend and colleague from UNHCR's now abandoned Kosovo office. She and her family were among the estimated 65,000 refugees now inhabiting the debris-strewn Blace fields. I froze with shock. Seeing Blerta, the helpful, well-traveled, eloquent woman who had been a mainstay in our Prishtinë / Priština office, in such horrible conditions suddenly brought home the tragedy that was unfolding before our eyes: my friend, my colleague was now a refugee.

The fields at Blace became known as "No-man's land", an incongruous description considering the mass of humanity that now jammed every square meter of available space. Many of the refugees had horrific stories to tell. The words gushed out in torrents as they struggled to come to grips with what had happened to them at the hands of the Yugoslav military and police. Many had witnessed their villages and homes being burned and their neighbours and relatives abused, abducted, or killed. Some had been forced to leave home at gunpoint. Others fled for fear of what might come if they stayed. Many headed for the border, having nowhere else to go, too frightened even to seek out relatives still inside Kosovo. Now, they anxiously inquired about missing family and friends, not knowing if they were alive or dead. The terror was palpable at Blace, and it was a scene that we knew was being repeated at border crossings all across southern and western Kosovo.

In 1998 and early 1999, UNHCR staff working inside Kosovo had witnessed the displacement of village after village. In a single day in early 1999, for example, more than 25,000 people were displaced because of heavy fighting in northwest and central Kosovo. Many went into hiding in forested areas, where they had no facilities or shelter. UNHCR staff would find and bring these displaced people to the nearest safer village or town. Other refugees had no choice but to remain in the woods, and tried to establish daily routines; in some places schools were even set up in the outdoors.

During the so-called cease-fire period from October 1998 to March 1999, the number of displaced people within Kosovo reached 260,000. We were constantly amazed by the generosity of the Kosovars who accepted the displaced into their homes as if they were family. On one occasion, a passing car stopped beside a UNHCR truck filled with people from the Kaçanik / Kačanik hills in southern Kosovo. Without hesitation, the driver of the car invited one of the displaced families to share his home. Asked about his generosity, the man said he was willing to help total strangers because his own family might soon face the same fate.

UNHCR, the OSCE and other agencies evacuated from Kosovo on March 23, 1999 – the day before the NATO air strikes began. Thereafter, in the absence of international observers and international humanitarian agencies, the violence and displacement within Kosovo intensified. It is still unclear exactly how many people were internally displaced during the months of the NATO campaign, but close to one million Kosovars, mostly Albanians, fled into the bordering areas of Albania, FYR Macedonia and Montenegro.

Albania, the poorest country in Europe, hosted the largest number of refugees, welcoming its ethnic brethren despite the huge economic burden. In the young nation of FYR Macedonia, founded only in 1991, the situation was more complex and the welcome initially frosty. The government expressed alarm at the prospect of tens of thousands of Albanian refugees converging and remaining on its territory and concern over maintaining the delicate balance between majority Macedonians and minority Albanians, the latter representing between 20 to 30% of the population.

For the tens of thousands of Kosovo Albanians being expelled from their homes, many forced onto trains or buses with absolutely no idea of their final destination, arrival at the Macedonian border initially brought new hope, but their ordeal was far from over. Many had to wait in insufferable queues at the border for up to sixteen hours at a stretch – withstanding bitter cold in the early spring and boiling heat later on - only to be prevented from moving from the border fields at Blace, where they had to cope with terrible sanitation, inadequate shelter and lack of aid. Others waited for up to five days on the Kosovo side but were refused exit by the Yugoslav authorities. Some had to return to Prishtinë / Priština, a terrifying journey under the circumstances.

With international concern mounting at the plight of the refugees, Macedonian authorities gradually became more open to offers of help. Following intense negotiations between international representatives and the Macedonian government, the huge crowd of 65,000 refugees that was packed into Blace's muddy fields in late March was eventually allowed to move onwards. Finally, the UN and international agencies were given access to Blace and were able to provide more support to the refugees by organising the whole area into a smaller transit site for potential newcomers. Some were then immediately transferred to Albania and Turkey on the basis of bilateral arrangements. Others were taken to new camps within FYR Macedonia that were rapidly being constructed by NATO troops. Eventually, some 245,000 made their way to FYR Macedonia, fleeing Yugoslav army and police actions in Kosovo. They found shelter with Albanian and Roma host families as well as in camps such as Stenkovec I and II.

The international community was sensitive to the concerns of the Macedonian government and anxious to prevent the refugee crisis from further destabilising the region. To help shoulder the burden, more than two dozen nations as far away as Australia volunteered to take part in a "Humanitarian Evacuation Programme" (HEP) organised by UNHCR and the International Organization for Migration. The programme eventually provided temporary refuge to nearly 100,000 people.

Many of those who remained in the camps and with host families in FYR Macedonia, Albania and Montenegro did so with the firm belief that they would soon return home. As spring moved toward summer, and the flow of refugees continued, this optimism sometimes seemed naïve and misplaced. Scores of humanitarian organisations and international NGOs set up programmes, scrambling to keep up with the influx. The sprawling Cegrane camp, which held over 40,000 refugees perched on a steep hillside south of Tetovo, was filled even before German troops could finish constructing it.

Life in the refugee camps was difficult and sometimes downright miserable. During times of heavy influx of people into FYR Macedonia, plastic sheeting was spread between tents to create shelter for the new arrivals until space could be found. Stretched to their breaking point, sewage systems and other infrastructure could not keep up, sparking fears of epidemics.

The prospect of spending the blazing Balkan summer in the very hot, crowded tented camps was a major worry for all who worked and live there. While struggling to find places for thousands of new arrivals, UNHCR and its partners also began preparations to winterise the camps lest the crisis drag on. Fortunately, following decisive efforts by international negotiators to secure agreements from the Yugoslav authorities to end the war, most refugees spent the following winter at home.

Today, nothing is left of the sprawling, dust-blown camps that once housed hundreds of thousands of desperate refugees. But for those who were there – refugees and aid workers alike – the memories of those chaotic days in the spring of 1999 remain all too vivid.

Paula Ghedini was the regional UNHCR spokesperson for Serbia, Montenegro and Kosovo from November 1998 to March 1999. She was then a spokesperson in FYR Macedonia until June 1999. Upon UNHCR return to Kosovo, she worked as a field officer in the Prishtinë / Priština region until October 1999, after which she resumed her post as a spokesperson for UNHCR in Kosovo until October 2000.

Kosovo Albanian refugees flee through the woods near Gajrë / Gajre where they had been hiding for three days since the Yugoslav army began shelling their villages. Most were forced to leave hastily with only a few belongings. An estimated 850,000 Albanians fled Kosovo in the spring of 1999. March 2, 1999. *Photo by Andrew Testa*

A policeman from Albania directs a wave of refugees crossing the border into Kukës. In total, 445,000 Kosovo Albanians found refuge in Albania during the crisis. April 1999. *Photo by Andrew Testa*

After several days of fleeing on foot through the woods near Gajrë / Gajre, these refugees were able to continue their journey by tractor. UNHCR later helped them move to a safer location in the village of Bob, near Kaçanik / Kačanik. March 2, 1999.
Photo by Andrew Testa

Albanians hide in the woods of the Shala Gorge in the Drenica region. They remained there for six weeks, until the conflict ended, under the protection of the Kosovo Liberation Army. Drenica was the first area to be completely controlled by KLA forces. During the NATO bombing campaign, schools were even established in some woodlands. June 1999. *Photo by Andrew Testa*

A Kosovo Albanian boy sleeps in the woods in the Kaçanik / Kačanik area. Many villagers were forced to hide out in the hills when the Yugoslav army increased attacks on civilians and intensified shelling of their homes. March 2, 1999. *Photo by Andrew Testa*

Refugees from Ferizaj / Uroševac wait in a bus at the Blace border. They are about to be transported to one of the refugee camps managed by UNHCR in FYR Macedonia. At the height of the refugee influx in April 1999, UNHCR estimated that up to 45,000 refugees arrived at the Blace border on a given day. April 1999. *Photo by Andrew Testa*

Exhausted refugees from Kosovo continue their journey into FYR Macedonia, using railway tracks as a path. The Yugoslav military had earlier deported them by train and confiscated money, jewelry, passports and identity cards of many passengers. Refugees were expected to pay for train or bus tickets. March 31, 1999. *Photo by Andrew Testa*

Refugees gather at Blace, the "no-man's land" at the Kosovo-FYR Macedonia border. Many people walked the entire way from Prishtinë / Priština to the border, while others who were more fortunate arrived on tractors or by cars. Some were denied exit by Yugoslav authorities and forced to turn back. Others had to wait for days to be given authorisation to enter FYR Macedonia. Within the first weeks of the crisis, only a very small number of NGOs were allowed access to the "no-man's land"; refugees subsisted with a few pieces of plastic sheeting over branches torn from trees. Some died under these conditions and were buried on the spot. April 1999.
Photo by Andrew Testa

Following international pressure, a more functional transition camp was later built at Blace under UNHCR management. Thousands of Kosovars continued to arrive daily and received assistance from UNHCR and its partners. Refugees spent between a day and a week there until the Macedonian authorities gave permission for entry and transported them to camps within the country. May 1999. *Photo by Andrew Testa*

Macedonian police watch as a Kosovo Albanian refugee carries her daughter into Raduša camp. The girl had collapsed from exhaustion by the side of the road. On a number of occasions, Kosovar refugees were only allowed to cross the border after UNHCR negotiated and formally appealed to the Macedonian government regarding its legal responsibilities to grant asylum to refugees within its borders. FYR Macedonia became a signatory of the 1951 UN Convention relating to the status of Refugees in 1994. April 16, 1999. *Photo by Andrew Testa*

A refugee from Kovaçevë / Kovačevac recovers from his ordeal. After his village was attacked and burned by Yugoslav forces, he trekked for two days through difficult mountain terrain to reach the border with FYR Macedonia. After an additional two days of walking, he took refuge in a mosque in the village of Odri, where he was discovered by police who then transported him to the refugee camp in Senokos, FYR Macedonia. May 1999. *Photo by Andrew Testa*

After spending a rainy night outside, a sixty-one year old woman from Podujevë / Podujevo seeks shelter under UNHCR plastic sheeting at the Cegrane refugee camp in FYR Macedonia. During the course of three consecutive nights, some 15,000 people arrived at the camp, making the demand for tents increasingly difficult to meet. May 1999. *Photo by Kael Alford*

A Kosovo Albanian boy sits on the hill overlooking the crowded camp of Stenkovec II, located between the capital city of Skopje and the Blace border. At its peak, around 24,000 refugees lived in the camp, which was originally planned for 4,000 people. After Albanians were able to return to Kosovo, it became a camp for Roma refugees. April 8, 1999. *Photo by Hazir Reka*

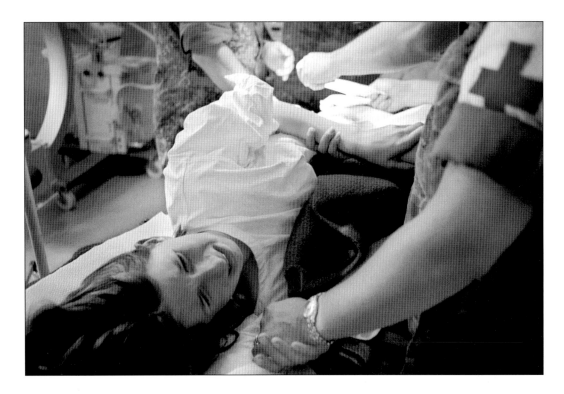

In the hospital run by the German army at Cegrane camp, Albiana has her bandages changed to protect a ten cen-timetre bullet wound. She was hit when her family, who had been hiding in the mountains for five weeks, came under fire from Yugoslav forces.

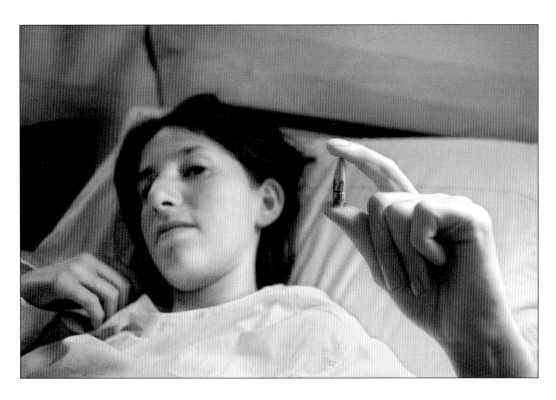

Albiana holds up the bullet that was removed from her hip. Two children from her family were wounded and Albiana's eleven year old cousin was killed in the attack. May 1999. *Photos by Kael Alford*

Merrushe holds a china tea cup that she salvaged from her house in Ferizaj / Uroševac before it was burned in 1998 by Yugoslav forces. Her family spent the following year staying at different places with friends in Kosovo before having to flee again during the NATO bombing campaign. They finally ended up in a camp at Stenkovec. "I wanted to take photos so my daughter could remember, but I didn't have time," said Merrushe. "So I took the cup as a reminder of everything from my life, just to have something from my home." May 1999. *Photo by Kael Alford*

A Kosovo Albanian woman gets a hand to help her prop up the plastic sheet sheltering her and other refugees from the rain near Morinë, at the Albanian border. May 1999. *Photo by Radhika Chalasani*

Two Kosovo sisters-in-law, having just arrived in Kukës as refugees, contemplate their next step in their new surroundings. Kukës is one of the most desperately poor parts of northern Albania. Refugees were eventually accommodated in UNHCR-run camps, with local families in their homes or sheltered in schools. May 1999. *Photo by Barron Rachman*

Kosovo Albanians queue for bread distribution in Kukës. UNHCR and other humanitarian agencies provided

food and other essential assistance to the refugees during the crisis. April 1999. *Photo by Andrew Testa*

Refugees at Stenkovec I camp say farewell to relatives and friends before being taken to various destinations in Western Europe, the United States and other countries under the Humanitarian Evacuation Programme. In co-ordination with UNHCR, twenty-nine countries took part in the HEP, which provided temporary asylum for approximately 90,000 refugees from Kosovo during the crisis. May 1999. *Photo by Andrew Testa*

Refugee children play together at Stenkovec II camp. Several international and local NGOs as well as international agencies, such as UNICEF, organised educational and recreational activities for the children in the camps inside FYR Macedonia. April 8, 1999.
Photo by Hazir Reka

Kosovo Albanian youths take a dip in the river near the Stenkovec refugee camps. After the first few weeks of terrible cold and rain, summer rapidly descended. The sun outside was scorching, and the shelter of canvas tents became hot and suffocating. Refugees were not allowed to go outside of the camps, and especially for the young people, some form of distraction was badly needed. Basketball games, coffee houses and workshops were eventually set up. May 1999. *Photo by Andrew Testa*

The Krasniqi family, from the Podujevë / Podujevo region, gather in their tent in the Stenkovec refugee camp. The family was ordered out of their house by police and managed to take only a videotape featuring the childrens' favourite uncles. The precious cassette was lost when the family transited through the Blace camp. May 9, 1999. *Photo by Kael Alford*

Refugees search the notice board at Stenkovec for news of relatives. The board was an innovation of the refugees to help them receive updated information about relatives and friends, as many families had been separated during their exodus. April 1999.
Photo by Andrew Testa

A thirty-four year old barber from Sllovi / Slovinje tries to recuperate in the German hospital inside Cegrane camp. He was shot by Serb paramilitaries while fleeing, after witnessing members of his family being killed. The bullet, still in his body when he arrived at Cegrane, was removed the following day. May 5, 1999. *Photo by Andrew Testa*

RETURN

Return

By Paula Ghedini

As the summer of 1999 approached and talk of a possible cease-fire in Yugoslavia began circulating, the mood among the hundreds of thousands of Kosovar refugees grew more hopeful by the day. Though home was just an hour or two up the road, most refugees had fled weeks earlier without knowing if they would ever be able to return. By early June, however, the uncertainty began to give way to optimism that soon the exile would end. Kumanovo, a town in the northern part of FYR Macedonia, momentarily became the center of world attention as talks were held between NATO and the Belgrade government on a cessation of hostilities. Following the military agreement that ended the conflict, the return of the refugees became a high priority on the international community's agenda.

On June 12, the first KFOR troops entered Kosovo, and Yugoslav army and police forces began their withdrawal. A day later, UNHCR led the return of international humanitarian agencies into Kosovo. After an absence of nearly three months, we had no idea what we would find on the other side of the border and approached the return with a mix of pride and anxiety. June 13 was a very long day. Early in the morning, slotted in between hundreds of KFOR military trucks, tanks, troop carriers and other heavy equipment, our fifty-vehicle UN convoy crept toward the border, passing camps where thousands of cheering refugees lined the roads. We became part of a huge line of vehicles that stretched from the Blace border all the way to Prishtinë / Priština, ninety kilometres to the north. Protected by helicopters overhead and troops and tanks in newly constructed roadside positions, we inched our way north through a largely abandoned landscape of smoldering houses and destroyed towns and villages. It was into this devastation that we would soon be helping refugees return.

Six hours later, we arrived in Prishtinë / Priština to find our office ransacked but the UNHCR warehouse still intact, guarded by a drunken civilian armed with an AK-47. The damage in the capital city itself was relatively light, although many apartments and houses had been extensively looted. The streets were deserted except for Yugoslav soldiers and police, who were not at all happy to see us. Immediately upon its return to Kosovo, UNHCR launched an information campaign urging refugees in Albania and FYR Macedonia to be patient and to give the humanitarian agencies a chance to get re-established. It would take time to resume operations, set up an aid distribution network, assess the damage and get started with land-mine clearance. But all of these things had to be done quickly so that the refugees could come home and start to rebuild as soon as possible.

It was often said that the Kosovo Albanians were among the most return-oriented refugees UNHCR had ever worked with. Even so, the size and speed of their return was amazing and unexpected. Largely ignoring pleas for restraint and warnings about mines, ongoing security risks and heavy destruction, they began flooding back to Kosovo by the hundreds of thousands. In fact, their spontaneous return was much swifter than their exodus. Many were so determined to get home that they went around and ahead of KFOR forces, taking side roads and shortcuts through the forests. UNHCR had prepared careful plans based on estimates of 400,000 returnees to Kosovo by September of 1999. Instead, more than 740,000 arrived home by the end of July. We were confronted with another major challenge: the race against time to get everyone prepared before the onset of winter.

The returning Kosovars enjoyed a degree of freedom they had not experienced for a long time and their joy at being home was contagious, but they also discovered their world in a shambles. Some found their homes looted but livable. They were the lucky ones. Others returned to nothing but piles of rubble. Homes had been burned. Farm animals were dead. Fields lay fallow, and some had been planted with mines. Shops were looted. Mosques and cemeteries were defaced and in some cases completely destroyed. Wells were contaminated, many with animal carcasses and human bodies. Hospitals were emptied of supplies and medicines. Schools were destroyed and even booby-trapped. But Kosovo Albanians, known for their self-reliance, managed to overcome their shock and grief and got down rapidly to the hard work of rebuilding their lives. The transformation in just a few short months in late 1999 was amazing.

However, the return shattered the last hope for many who sought missing loved ones. They could no longer maintain the illusion that their friends and relatives might have been in another camp, in another country, or hiding out in the hills. Attention now turned to the missing, the mass graves and the lists of political prisoners known to have been transferred to Serbia. The tireless work of UNMIK, ICTY, ICRC and others to determine the fate of all those who are still missing from the Kosovo conflict will continue for years.

As that first winter approached, UNHCR and its partners worked to ensure that everyone would have basic shelter and assistance. Some 120,000 houses had been damaged or totally destroyed. Most schools, hospitals, power and water plants were in need of immediate repair. Food supplies were extremely low and agricultural production was minimal. During that time, WFP provided food to over 1.3 million people, more than half of the entire population of Kosovo.

UNHCR coordinated a large winter relief operation involving more than three hundred international agencies and NGOs – working on a dizzying array of projects benefiting hundreds of thousands of people. Thousands of tons of shelter materials were distributed, ensuring that people would have at least one weatherproof room in their damaged homes. Food rations for up to four months were provided to remote villages, along with other winter supplies like stoves, heating fuel, blankets and clothing. Schools and medical clinics were winterised and emergency accommodation centres identified and stocked with supplies. In the end, it was a difficult winter, but no one died of exposure and there were no epidemics.

Today, the reconstruction continues and a veneer of normalcy has returned to most towns and villages. Cafés are crowded and young people now stroll Prishtinë / Priština's Mother Teresa Street, a simple pleasure once denied them.

A boy plays with a clock in the centre of Gjakovë / Djakovica, a town that was repeatedly hit by heavy shelling in 1999. More than 120,000 houses in Kosovo were seriously damaged or destroyed during the entire conflict. June 1999. *Photo by Radhika Chalasani*

Faced with the prospect of a bleak winter, Vetime comforts her tearful eleven year old daughter Arlanda, in front of their destroyed house in Medvexhë / Medvedje, Kosovo. The family fled their village on March 27, 1999, and found safety in Durrës, Albania, where they remained until the end of the war. June 1999. *Photo by Radhika Chalasani*

A Turkish KFOR soldier is joyfully welcomed as a liberator in Prizren in June 1999. Over 40,000 NATO troops were deployed in Kosovo just after the war ended. *Photo by Radhika Chalasani*

Samadrexhë / Samodraža is one of the many villages in Kosovo which was shelled during security forces' offensives in 1998 and again attacked by the Yugoslav military during the NATO campaign in 1999. When refugees came back to Kosovo at the end of the war, little was left of their houses. UNHCR provided humanitarian assistance for those who did not have a home anymore. June 18, 1999. *Photo by Hazir Reka*

A refugee retrieves the belongings he and his family had hidden in the mountains outside Studenicë / Studenica several months earlier, before escaping to Montenegro. Approximately 70,000 Kosovo Albanians were refugees in Montenegro during the conflict. July 1999. *Photo by Barron Rachman*

Several days after their return to Kosovo, two young men dig up the body of their grandfather. The old man was forced to come out of hiding in the mountains near Studenicë / Studenica to gather food for his family but was shot by Serb paramilitaries on the way back to his home. In the two years following the conflict, 3,623 bodies, most of them of ethnic Albanians, have been exhumed by ICTY from 520 gravesites throughout Kosovo. July 1999. *Photo by Barron Rachman*

A woman who lost more than a dozen family members in a massacre by Yugoslav police on March 17, 1999, visits the site of the killing, in the village of Poklek i Vjetër / Stari Poklek. Police forced the villagers in a room of the house and threw in grenades and fired automatic rifles at the captives, killing fifty-four people, twenty-four of them children and including a six-month-old baby. October 28, 2000. *Photo by Kael Alford*

One of the many mass grave sites now found in Kosovo. In February 1998, one of the most brutal massacres took place in Çirez / Čirez and Likoshan / Likošane, in the Drenica region. Over 10,000 Albanians, including civilians and combattants, are believed to have been killed throughout Kosovo from February 1998 to June 1999. February 2000. *Photo by Hélène Caux*

The former post office in Prishtinë / Priština. The building was used by Yugoslav police and army as a telecommunications base, before being destroyed by NATO during the bombing campaign. October 1999.
Photo by Hélène Caux

While Albanian refugees returned home, a new exodus began. A convoy of Serb vehicles, packed to overflowing with personal belongings, leaves Uroševac / Ferizaj and heads slowly towards Serbia. KFOR escorted to safety many convoys of Serbs to the Serbian boundary during the summer of 1999. Approximately 150,000 non-Albanians fled Kosovo in the immediate aftermath of the war. June 17, 1999.
Photo by Hazir Reka

Mourners heading for the cemetery in the village of Staro Gracko / Grackë e Vjetër are escorted by British KFOR soldiers. Hundreds of people gathered to bury fourteen Serb farmers who were murdered while working in their fields - one of the worst atrocities committed in Kosovo after the arrival of NATO-led peacekeepers. July 28, 1999. *Photo by Hazir Reka*

Bystanders watch a house in Priština / Prishtinë go up in flames. Upon the return of the Albanian refugees to Kosovo, many Serb, Roma and Ashkaelia houses were burned on a daily basis during the summer of 1999. June 1999. *Photo by Hazir Reka*

Birds fly over a Prishtinë / Priština suburb. The flocks of blackbirds coming home to roost are a powerful and emotional vision each day for Kosovars and international workers. January 2000. *Photo by Andrew Testa*

After surveying the completely burned-out upper floor of her house in Viti / Vitina, Shqipe slowly walks down the staircase, one of the few remaining structures of her home. Many thousands of refugees temporarily stayed in tents, collective centres or with friends when they came back to Kosovo, as their houses had been seriously damaged or destroyed during the conflict. July 1999.
Photo by Hélène Caux

The family of a sixteen year old Catholic Albanian boy mourn his death at his funeral in Dollc / Dolac village. The teenager had stepped on a landmine while collecting fruit near the Montenegrin boundary, which was heavily mined. According to the UN Mine Action Co-ordination Centre (UNMACC), 87 people were killed and 357 people injured by landmines or unexploded cluster bombs between June 1999 and October 2001. July 1999. *Photo by Kael Alford*

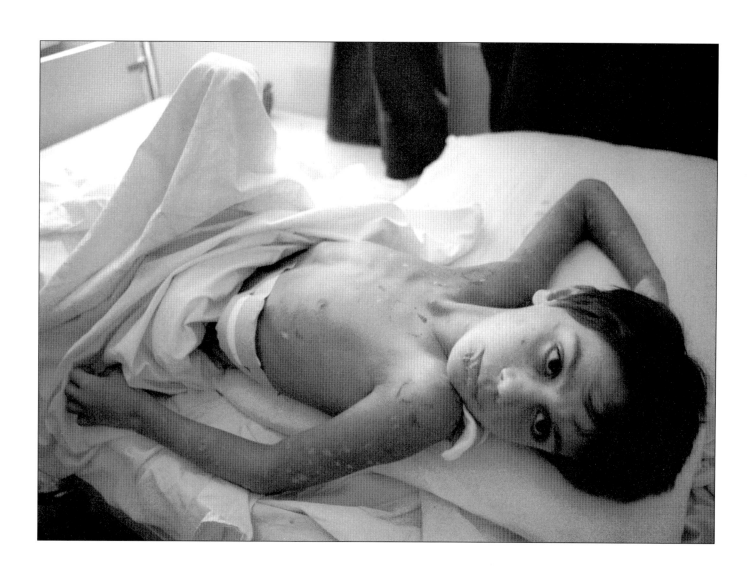

A Roma boy lies injured, the casualty of a NATO cluster bomb that landed unexploded in the hills close to his home near Gjakovë / Djakovica. The boy was standing less than two metres away when the bomb detonated in the hands of a neighbour who was scraping dirt off the cartridge with a knife. Three people were killed in the blast, including a nine year old boy. August 4, 1999.
Photo by Kael Alford

A child peers through the wall of what used to be his home in the north of Kosovo. Similar destruction of property belonging to people of all ethnicities has occurred throughout Kosovo before, during and in the aftermath of the conflict, leaving hundreds of thousands of people destitute and dependant on others. September 2000.
Photo by Hélène Caux

In a transit camp in Mitrovicë / Mitrovica, children and their families improvise games to play with plastic sheeting. After the war, they arrived home from refugee camps in FYR Macedonia and Albania to find their houses destroyed. They stayed in the transit centre for several days until UNHCR and the NGO ADRA helped them find accommodation in collective centres or with relatives and friends. September 1999. *Photo by Hélène Caux*

Agnesa and her family escaped Kosovo in April 1999 and stayed more than two months in a refugee camp in Albania. When they returned to Suhodolli i Epërm / Suvi Do, they found their home had been partly destroyed by arson. UNHCR provided them with tents until repairs could be completed. August 1999. *Photo by Hélène Caux*

Several international organisations, including the European Community Humanitarian Office (ECHO) and various NGOs distributed wood to help families - like here in Klinë / Klina - to heat their homes during the harsh winter of 1999-2000. In mountain villages, temperatures frequently dropped to –30°C. Wood distribution continued throughout the following winters. Stoves and coal were also given to help villagers cope with the cold. November 2000. *Photo by Hélène Caux*

The Winter Emergency Team was set up by UNHCR to fill the gaps of humanitarian assistance, particularly in remote areas of Kosovo. With the help of KFOR, members of the team regularly flew by helicopter to villages in the mountains north of Mitrovicë / Mitrovica where they distributed assistance items, including food and winter supplies.

The UNHCR warehouse in Prishtinë / Priština, where mattresses, blankets and sleeping bags are stored before being distributed to families whose possessions were destroyed during the war.

A young boy in the mountains around Prizren, with UNHCR packages containing hygienic items, a stove and other kitchen wares.

Kosovo Albanians rebuilding their house for the winter in Vasilevë / Vasiljevo. UNHCR distributed shelter kits containing roof beams, plastic sheeting, and tools so that people could secure at least one warm and weather-proof room before the winter.

October 1999. *Photos by Hélène Caux*

The end of the war brought another tragedy to the forefront as the search for missing people began in earnest. The city of Gjakovë / Djakovica was particularly affected and its population organised regular demonstrations to pressure Serbian authorities to release Kosovo Albanians still being detained in Serbian jails. The role of UNMIK and ICRC was crucial in facilitating the release of hundreds of prisoners. As of October 30, 2001, 3587 Kosovars were still reported as missing. February 2000. *Photo by Hélène Caux*

An Albanian is greeted by relatives after being released in Merdar / Merdare, at the Kosovo - Serbia boundary, along with thirty other men and women. All of them had been detained at Požarevac prison in Serbia, which in November 2001 continued to hold Albanian prisoners. April 21, 2000. *Photo by Andrew Testa*

Gjakovë / Djakovica was heavily targeted by the Yugoslav army during the conflict, and many Albanian homes and shops were burned. This image of one of the city's main arteries is indicative of the tremendous level of destruction. October 1999. *Photo by Hélène Caux*

A man rides his bicycle past the ruins of a shop as workers begin to rebuild it. Gjakovicë / Djakovica is famous for its mercantile spirit, but businesses reopened very slowly after the war due to the high number of casualties among the male population. Reconstruction in the main shopping district began on the first anniversary of its destruction. March 19, 2000. *Photo by Kael Alford*

A free-spirited cow caught in mid-day traffic in Prishtinë / Priština. Thousands of animals were killed during the conflict, leaving farmers without livestock when they returned to Kosovo. Between September 1999 and October 2000, the government of Switzerland flew in about 1,700 head of cattle to help revive the farming sector. They were distributed to vulnerable families and the cows soon gave birth to over a thousand calves. August 2000. *Photo by Hélène Caux*

Girls celebrate their first day back at school in Dardania, Prishtinë / Priština. Albanian children were effectively excluded from schools in 1990. In order to be able to study in their own language, they had to continue their lessons in a parallel system of education held in private housing throughout Kosovo. September 1, 1999. *Photo by Hazir Reka*

A fifty-six year old man cuts the grass of his garden in Graboc i Epërm / Gornji Grabovac in a sign of increasing normality in Kosovo. The ruins of his house remain a stark reminder of the events of 1999. May 2000. *Photo by Andrew Testa*

When Delfina returned to Kosovo from Montenegro, where she had been a refugee during the 1999 war, she was hired as a deminer by the NGO Norwegian People's Aid. Although her family and friends discouraged her from taking the job because it was seen as inappropriate for a woman, Delfina became the supervisor of an all-women demining platoon. Her team worked throughout the spring and summer seasons in the heavily mined region of Pejë / Peć. "I decided to do this job after seeing pictures of children who had been victims of mine incidents, it was just too overwhelming", Delfina says. August 2000. *Photo by Hélène Caux*

Most of the men and boys from Krushë e Vogël / Mala Kruša were massacred by Yugoslav military in March 1999. Many of the women have therefore become de facto heads of family and taken responsibility for work previously performed by men, in addition to caring for their homes and children. Fifteen women from the village completed a driving course organised by the NGO Motrat Qiriazi and funded by UNHCR Kosovo Women's Initiative and are now using tractors for agricultural work. October 2000.
Photo by Hélène Caux

A holiday portrait taken on the eve of the millenium with Santa Claus and a princess in Prishtinë / Priština. December 1999.
Photo by Hélène Caux

ENCLAVES

Enclaves

By Grainne O'Hara

In its early stages, the Kosovo crisis was one of the most filmed and photographed calamities of the twentieth century. The international media doled out a daily ration of human misery, in the form of excruciatingly detailed coverage that nagged at our collective conscience. Ethnic violence, an evil perfected in the Balkans over the previous disastrous decade, was once again ravaging the countryside. Its primary target this time: the Kosovo Albanians.

Thanks to this coverage, in the minds of much of the public, Kosovo seemed a brief but intense struggle of good versus evil. The Kosovo Albanians were seen as innocent victims valiantly defying their Serb oppressors. Finally, an outraged international community came to their rescue. But part of the tragedy of Kosovo is that neither the drama nor the oppression ended with the withdrawal of Yugoslav forces in mid-June 1999. The plight of the ethnic Albanians is indeed a large part of the recent story of Kosovo. But to leave it there is to leave untold a tragic story of human misery that continues to this day. Suffering and displacement are not exclusive to Kosovo Albanians. The harsh reality is that no ethnic group has been spared. All of them have been affected to some degree.

Contrary to popular perception, Kosovo is not simply a place inhabited by good Albanians and bad Serbs - or vice versa. The members of a third group, the Roma, unhappily sandwiched in between, have been variously cast as misguided opportunists or willing collaborators. And the mosaic is yet more complex: Kosovo is home to a multitude of ethnic groups. Albanians and Serbs live alongside not just Roma, but also Gorani, Torbeshi, Cherkezi, Turks, Bosniaks, Croats, and ethnic groups that are little known to the outside world, including "Egyptians" and Ashkaelia, who have often been misidentified as Roma. Although many of these communities trace their distant origins elsewhere, they all call Kosovo home. It is a home they cherish, and one which they will not easily relinquish - even in the face of the violence that continues to confront them.

The departure of Kosovo´s minorities began in the spring of 1999, but was largely overshadowed by the dramatic flight of hundreds of thousands of Albanians. Ashkaelia and Egyptians joined this first exodus during the NATO airstrikes, often fleeing alongside the Albanians with whom they had already shared months of internal displacement and hardship. The various groups' ties of common daily experience were strengthened in many cases by a shared language and religion.

In the refugee camps of neighbouring FYR Macedonia, there was initially no need to separate refugees along ethnic lines. Sadly, however, the mistrust that has split ethnic communities throughout the Balkans eventually became obvious there as well. Reports of Roma collaboration with the Serbs in Kosovo began filtering across the border, often brought by newly arrived groups of refugees. Soon, the sins of a few were being attributed to all Roma. In early June, riots erupted in FYR Macedonia's Stenkovec camps and minorities were from then on segregated – despite their protestations of innocence from the crimes committed by the Yugoslav army and police against the Albanians.

In mid-June, hundreds of thousands of Albanians rushed back to a devastated Kosovo. But the Roma, despite their strong desire to return home, quickly became the sole inhabitants of the refugee camps. Those who dared to return were soon back in the camps with shocking tales of abuse by their former Albanian neighbours. Burnings, beatings and even killings left no doubt that for now, there was to be no joyous return, no hopeful homecoming for the Roma.

Since the establishment of the United Nations Interim Administration Mission in Kosovo (UNMIK) in June of 1999, an estimated one million Albanians have returned home. However, during the immediate months that followed, more than 150,000* members of various minority communities abandoned their homes, in fear for their lives. Many fled for an uncertain future in the refugee camps and collective centres for displaced persons that seem to have become a permanent feature of the Balkans. This includes Serbs, who left in the tens of thousands, most of them close on the heels of the withdrawing Yugoslav army after June 12. Their convoys of cars and tractors, piled high with belongings, were a tragic mirror image of the Albanians who had themselves fled only months before.

The outside world was shocked by reports of continuing violence - this time perpetrated by the Albanians. Such scenes were not part of the script, which was supposed to end happily with the restoration of a multi-ethnic Kosovo. Instead, many minority homes were put to the torch by angry groups bent on revenge. Serb and other minority families were attacked within their own homes and when venturing out in public, ranging from physical assault to hand-grenade attacks and shootings. For many, threats of violence or of expulsion from their homes was enough to prompt their fearful departure. Many of those who remained in Kosovo ended up living in enclaves heavily guarded by KFOR.

The provision of basic services like healthcare and education to people isolated in these enclaves has become a complex challenge. To include minority populations in mainstream society requires a degree of commitment, flexibility and imagination that the international community has found difficult to master and that large segments of the Albanian population often reject.

Lack of freedom of movement is one of the harsh realities of enclave life, preventing minorities from doing many of the everyday activities most of us take for granted. To ensure this most basic of human rights, UNHCR introduced special bus lines for regular travel in and out of the enclaves. Passengers relish the chance to escape the tension ridden monotony of enclave life – to shop, to go to the doctor, to visit friends or simply to go for a walk in different surroundings. To witness the pre-boarding excitement, tinged with apprehension and sadness in an enclave like upper Orahovac / Rahovec, is to know something of the value of this seemingly simple service. To witness the disdain and the threatening gestures of some of the Albanians as the buses roll through town is to know something of the fear that minority populations live with daily.

* According to UNHCR official registration, by late 2001, more than 230 000 people from Kosovo were displaced in Serbia and Montenegro.

Painted white and with UNHCR emblazoned on the side in distinctive blue lettering, all the buses operate under KFOR armed escort. Stoning, insults and threatening gestures are common, but no one was prepared for the vicious attack on February 2, 2000, when rocket-propelled grenades ripped through one of the buses outside of Mitrovica / Mitrovicë. Two Serb passengers were killed and the entire transportation programme was immediately suspended. It took almost three months and a major review of security arrangements before all the bus lines would resume service.

Serbs may have borne the brunt of Kosovo's post-war violence, but in fact no minority group remains untouched. In many areas of Kosovo, Bosniaks and other Muslim Slavs no longer dare to speak their language in public. A dwindling Croat population wonders how their community will fit into an Albanian-dominated society. Kosovo's Turkish population has been angered and disappointed at the failure of the international community to recognise theirs as one of the official languages of the new administration. Many have left, abandoning their homes, churches, mosques and communities.

Kosovo Albanians, too, continue to suffer the hardships of exclusion and isolation. In northern Kosovo, where Serbs are in the majority, Albanians live under constant threat of violent attacks and displacement. In the northern part of Mitrovicë / Mitrovica for instance, three tower blocks inhabited by some remaining Albanians are constantly under KFOR guard. Other people have yet to return to their homes there: Roma who used to live in the south part of the city found that their neighbourhood was completely burned when Albanians came back from exile in June 1999. Some of these Roma now live in prefabricated houses by the railway in the northern part of the city.

For those who want to consider return, UNHCR arranges, with the help of KFOR, "go-and-see" visits and provides as much information on the conditions of daily life, particularly on security, as possible. For Serbs and other minorities, return to certain areas of Kosovo has already started, although very slowly and in very small numbers. UNHCR continues to work for the voluntary return of all Kosovars to their original homes, and efforts are being made to create a safer place for all ethnicities in Kosovo. But the prospect of return is still very uncertain, paved with numerous obstacles such as the ongoing violence, the destruction or occupation of the homes of potential returnees, and surrounding hostility. Among the signs of hope are the multi-ethnic projects, including some sponsored by local NGOs, that have been initiated since 1999, and although they remain on a small scale, they certainly are an indication that there is a will, for some, to live together.

The story of Kosovo did not end in the summer of 1999. Its minority population continues to suffer. Kosovo is their home, too. The plight of those who are still displaced, as well as those who struggle to remain in Kosovo, also deserves the world's attention, but ultimately only the Kosovars themselves can decide to make Kosovo once again a home for all its people.

Grainne O'Hara is a protection officer for UNHCR. She worked in FYR Macedonia from April to October 1999, and then in Kosovo until November 2001.

Roma and Ashkaelia girls observing the camera, a diversion from games usually played in the confined playground of their enclosed camp in Kruševac / Krushec. By July 1999, more than a thousand Roma and Ashkaelia had sought refuge in a school in Kosovo Polje / Fushë Kosovë. This followed revenge attacks by Albanians who believed Roma had collaborated in crimes against them during the NATO bombing. UNHCR later moved the Roma and Ashkaelia to a tented facility in Kruševac / Krushec. December 1999. *Photo by Hélène Caux*

Kosovo Serb women drive away in distress from what has become an enclaved area in Orahovac / Rahovec. They travel to a more secure environment in Serbia. Restrictions on their movement outside the enclave and their general fear led them, like many other Serbs, to leave Kosovo in the months after the war ended. A similar convoy en route to Montenegro was attacked by Albanians who were in the streets when the line of cars and buses passed through the town of Peć / Pejë. October 1999.
Photo by Andrew Testa

The entrance to the Serb enclave of Goraždevac / Gorazhdec is guarded around the clock by KFOR soldiers. The main road, which is generally calm during the day, is also used by Albanians, as it is the only route for them to reach their villages, but their passage through Goraždevac / Gorazhdec sometimes stirs tensions among the Serb population. June 2000. *Photo by Kael Alford*

Albanians walk across the main bridge that divides Mitrovicë / Mitrovica, where there is a Serb majority in the north and an Albanian majority in the south. These Albanians had fled their homes in the north after an outbreak of violence at the beginning of February, 2000, but following an intervention by British KFOR to restore calm in the area, were soon able to return to their apartments. The situation in the divided town remains volatile, with continued tensions between the different ethnic communities in both sections of the city. February 2000. *Photo by Andrew Testa*

This Albanian father never goes out except to take his daughter to school. They both live at his brother's home, in north Mitrovicë / Mitrovica, after being expelled from their home - now occupied by Serbs - in Zveçan / Zvečan. Serbs frequently harass the little girl and her family, knocking at the door of their apartment and insulting them. September 2000.
Photo by Hélène Caux

Albanian children cross from their homes in northern Mitrovicë / Mitrovica to school in the south. Some Albanians remaining in the Serb dominated north live in three tower blocks by the river Ibar. They are able to cross safely into the Albanian south, by using a foot-bridge constructed by French KFOR. September 2000.
Photo by Hélène Caux

A four-year old Roma boy proudly wears his father's shoes in the mud and rain at Kruševac / Krushec camp. UNHCR and its partner, the NGO Italian Consortium for Solidarity (ICS), administered the camp until improved accomodation could be devised. December 1999. *Photo by Hélène Caux*

Against the backdrop of the Obiliq / Obilić power plant, a Roma family travels by horsecart to the heated winter barracks in Plemetina / Plemetin. In December 1999, UNHCR, the Danish Refugee Council (DRC) and ICS helped move around nine hundred Roma and Ashkaelia from tents in Kruševac / Krushec to heated barracks in Plemetina / Plemetin.
Photo by Hélène Caux

Despite difficult living conditions, children find ways to play in the Plemetina / Plemetin camp. March 2000.
Photo by Hélène Caux

View out of the window of a hairdressing workshop run by women at the Plemetina / Plemetin camp. A mural has been painted on the wall of the community center and library building opposite. One of the few positive things to come out of the camp environment has been the establishment of a basic school system by the Roma and Ashkaelia themselves. About eighty children from seven to eleven years old regularly attend the school. March 2000. *Photo by Hélène Caux*

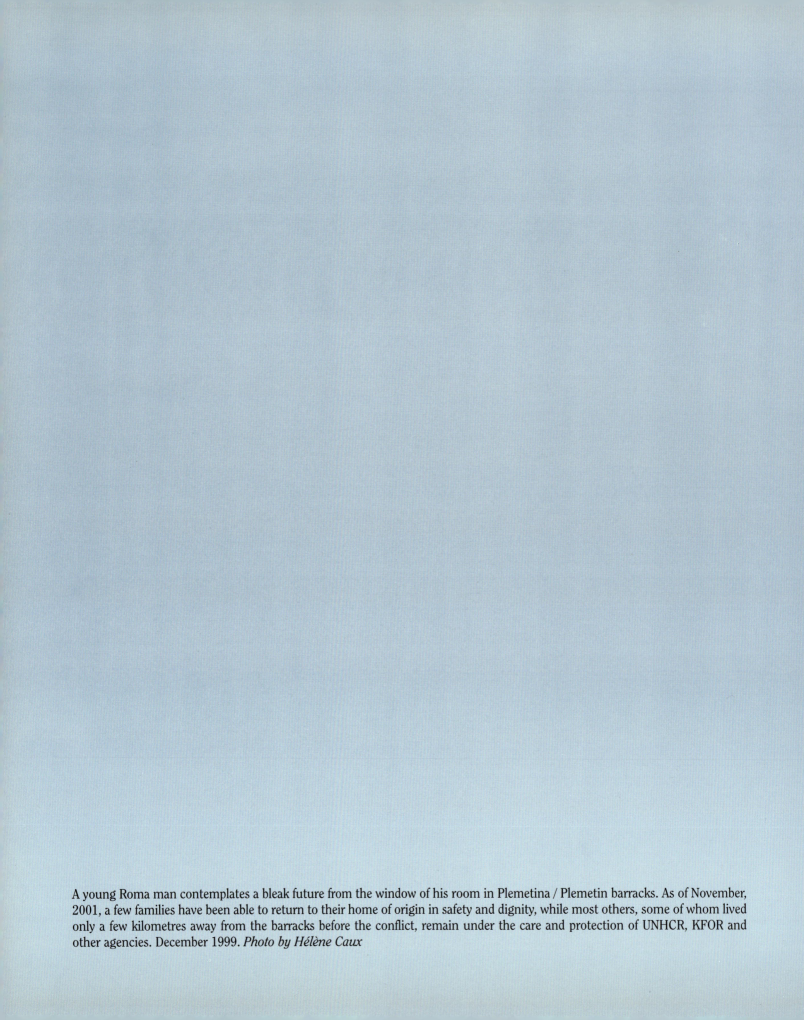

A young Roma man contemplates a bleak future from the window of his room in Plemetina / Plemetin barracks. As of November, 2001, a few families have been able to return to their home of origin in safety and dignity, while most others, some of whom lived only a few kilometres away from the barracks before the conflict, remain under the care and protection of UNHCR, KFOR and other agencies. December 1999. *Photo by Hélène Caux*

In Gnjilane / Gjilan a Serb woman greets friends before boarding the UNHCR bus to visit relatives in a nearby village. The UNHCR bus service was aimed at increasing freedom of movement for minorities and was managed by the Danish Refugee Council with armed KFOR escorts. Since June 2001, the project has been run under the auspices of UNMIK. For many, the buses represent the only opportunity to connect with family and friends, to visit the doctor or to go shopping. October 1999. *Photo by Hélène Caux*

Women grieve at the funeral of three Kosovo Egyptians murdered in an attack triggered by a land dispute in Prishtinë / Priština area. In October 1999, some Albanians attempted to appropriate the land of an Egyptian family, and in the ensuing fight, two of the attackers were killed. Seven months later, an eighty year old man and his two grandsons, ages fifteen and sixteen, were shot dead as they returned home from a nearby shop. April 2000. *Photo by Andrew Testa*

On February 2, 2000, a clearly marked UNHCR bus was attacked by a rocket-propelled grenade outside of Mitrovica / Mitrovicë. Two Serb passengers were killed. As a result, all UNHCR bus lines in Kosovo were temporarily suspended, and it took almost three months to restore services. It was the only time in the history of UNHCR that one of its buses used for humanitarian purposes was so violently attacked. *Photos by Hélène Caux*

Kosovo Serbs board a train at a station near Vučitrn / Vushtrri. The train, which operates under KFOR protection from Prishtinë / Priština to Zveçan / Zvečan, is one of the few ways for Serbs and Roma to travel safely through Kosovo. Despite such security measures, the windows of the train have been repeatedly shattered by stones thrown by Albanians. KFOR's attempts to employ Albanian conductors on the train provoked similar stone throwing by the Serbs. October 15, 2000. *Photo by Andrew Testa*

A UNHCR organised "go and see" visit for Kosovo Serbs still displaced in Serbia. For many, it was the first time they returned to their homes in Kosovo since the end of the war, and some found that their houses had been destroyed. KFOR provides security during these "go and see" visits.

A Kosovo Serb, displaced in Serbia since June 1999, travels in a KFOR truck to visit his house in the Peć / Pejë area. Such visits offer displaced people an opportunity to see the actual situation on the ground for themselves, in order to make a more informed decision about whether or not to return to Kosovo. August 2000. *Photos by Hélène Caux*

Kosovo Serbs prepare to board a KFOR truck in Orahovac / Rahovec en route to taking the weekly UNHCR bus to Zvečan / Zveçan.
Serbs and Roma live in an enclave within the city where the majority of inhabitants are Albanians. August 2000.
Photo by Hélène Caux

The Orthodox seminary in Prizren continues to provide accommodation for a
few displaced Serbs and Roma who
sought refuge after they fled their
homes in the summer of 1999. They rely
on UNHCR and international NGOs to
bring them regular assistance as they
are still not able to venture safely outside the walls of the seminary, which is
guarded by KFOR. April 2000.
Photo by Hélène Caux

The coffins of four Ashkaelia men, who had been displaced to Fushë Kosovë / Kosovo Polje at the end of the war. Two days after they returned to their village of origin in Dashec / Doševac in November 2000, their dead bodies were discovered near the tents where they had been sleeping. The international community and various Albanian leaders, including Adem Demaçi - Chairman of the Committee for Well-Understanding, Tolerance and Co-existence - attended the burial in Fushë Kosovë / Kosovo Polje, and strongly condemned the savage murders. A seventeen year old teenager was among the victims. November 15, 2000.
Photo by Hélène Caux

An old woman and her cow, in Letnica / Letnicë. Care of livestock is traditionally undertaken by women in this village. Only sixty-five of the 780 Croats who lived there in the 1990s remain today. They now share the village with Catholic Albanians. There are around 400 Croats still living in Kosovo, compared to some 9,000 before the 1999 war. March 2000. *Photo by Hélène Caux*

Approximately 380 displaced Roma people from Kosovo are crowded into a sports hall in Belgrade. Accused by some Albanians of collaborating with the Serbs during the 1999 conflict, many had little choice but to leave Kosovo. Even though the families have put up blankets as makeshift dividers, privacy remains limited. Most Roma in this centre survive solely on humanitarian assistance. December 2000.
Photo by Hélène Caux

Kosovo Serbs waiting for lunch in a hotel turned collective centre near Belgrade. Most of them are displaced from Suva Reka / Suharekë. UNHCR provides heating fuel and food during the winter. Serbia is host to some 198,000 displaced persons from Kosovo – including Serbs and Romas - as well as 378,000 refugees from Bosnia-Herzegovina and Croatia. December 2000.
Photo by Hélène Caux

Roma children play by a garbage dump at the Konick camp in the outskirts of Podgorica, Montenegro. The camp provides accomodation for some 1,800 Roma and Egyptians, who fled Kosovo at the end of the war. Many have since expressed an interest in going back to their homes in Kosovo. Assistance in the camp is provided by UNHCR and Italian NGO partner Intersos. July 2001.
Photo by Hélène Caux

A worshiper in the mosque in Mamushë / Mamuša. This village and others in the Prizren region have a predominantly Turkish population. In most places in Kosovo, mosques are attended by both Turks and Albanians. Turks have managed to keep their cultural and religious traditions strong, but are still lobbying, as a minority group, to have their language recognised as an official one in the new Kosovo. September 2000. *Photo by Hélène Caux*

Elsada, a Gorani, fled Kosovo with her family in April 1999, and found refuge in Bosnia. Like many non-Albanians, she still does not feel it is safe to return to Kosovo. In the single room she shares with her husband in a camp near Sarajevo, she has nostalgically drawn the minarets of the mosques in Prizren, the city where she was born and spent all her life until the war. July 2001.
Photo by Hélène Caux

An Ashakaelia woman works on rebuilding her house in the outskirts of Prishtinë / Priština. Her family and others were able to go back home before the winter of 2001, as part of a UNHCR organised return project. The housing reconstruction was funded by the Swedish government. The returnees had been displaced in Plemetin / Plemetina camp since July, 1999.

Reconstruction of a Serb house in the ethnically mixed village of Leshtar / Lještar, in the east of Kosovo. Both Albanian and Serb residents were displaced during and after the 1999 war and came back to rebuild their houses after agreeing to live together again. October 2001. *Photos by Hélène Caux*

A magician from Vermont, USA, performs for the kids in Plemetin / Plemetina camp, a moment of distracting entertainment within the boundaries of the camp. October 2001. *Photos by Hélène Caux.*

Epilogue

During the period that is visually documented in "A Journey Home", Kosovo has experienced a dramatic transformation. The post-war phase has ushered in profound changes to its physical, political, cultural, socio-economic and human landscape. However, the most fundamental change has not yet taken place. The human rights of many of Kosovo's people continue to be violated in the most brutal and pointless manner. All forms of violence are inter-connected and they permeate all spheres of society: domestic and sexual violence, political violence, ethnically motivated attacks on minorities, settling of scores and revenge. When the security and freedom of some are compromised, the whole of society is threatened.

Kosovo's ethnic minorities continue to live in fear, as incidents of harassment, intimidation, expulsions, expropriation or destruction of property, assault and even murder are commonplace. Most are confined to enclaves, their lives characterised by uncertainty over their communities' future. Albanians also remain under constant threat in the Serb-dominated areas of the North. A displaced population numbering hundreds of thousands waits in Serbia and Montenegro, unable to return and dispossessed of home and land without compensation. The justification for such realities to persist in a forward looking and modern Kosovo is wearing thin, and have become painful reminders of the perpetuation of violence…'Today is them, tomorrow it could be us again'. This cycle must be broken to free Kosovo from fear; only then can a peaceful transition into the 21st century begin.

Equally the right to return of refugees from outside Kosovo must be honoured to allow peace and stability to endure within and beyond its borders. Around 10,000 Albanian refugees from FYR Macedonia remain in Kosovo, of the 80,000 that fled conflict in 2001. Their arrival in Kosovo affected the delicate balance between majority and minorities achieved in some areas close to the border. This new exodus brought back painful memories to those who had lived as refugees two years earlier. The solidarity and empathy showed by Kosovo Albanians towards the newcomers was an example of great humanity and kindness. This humanity could and should be shared with other communities in Kosovo to increase the peace dividends that must benefit all.

In a society where war is commemorated by the majority as having brought freedom, and where the martyrdom, sacrifice and heroism of national struggle are celebrated, pacifism may seem unfashionable. It takes courage to challenge violence and reach out to those in need, when painful memories of death and loss may tempt us to look the other way. But some brave individuals and groups in Kosovo, such as the Committee for Well-understanding, Tolerance and Co-existence, KWI's multi-ethnic Councils and Kosova Women's Network, are doing just that, while many local women's NGOs have multi-ethnic membership and offer services to all communities, regardless of ethnicity, nationality or religion.

"A Journey Home" documents a pilgrimage of pain, duress, sadness and loss but also one of hope, return, fresh starts and new beginnings. The exodus of many of the photographed came to an end in June-July 1999 when they returned home. However, the toughest journey lay ahead. The bumpy road to peace was then, and still is, open to all the peoples of Kosovo. Let these images be a cautionary reminder to those who do not wish to walk it, and an encouragement to those who are already well on their way.

Igballe Rogova, the programme manager of the Albanian NGO Motrat Qiriazi (MQ), working with Nena, a Serbian woman. MQ is a local NGO created in 1990, providing support for rural women of all ethnicities in Kosovo. Projects mainly include capacity building of local women's groups as well as advocacy for women's rights. Igballe and Nena are working together to help establish programmes for women, regardless of their ethnicities. December 2000. *Photo by Hélène Caux*

Albanian lawyers from Norma Women's Association teaching women's rights issues to Ashkaelia in Fushë Kosovë / Kosovo Polje. Albanian women's NGOs are leading the way in working across the ethnic divides. June 2001. *Photo by Hélène Caux*

Two journalists work in their studio at *Radio Blue Sky*, the station run by the UN that presents news and magazines in Albanian, Serbian and Turkish. The staff in each of the three language teams work closely together to write and produce quality programmes. The women are seen here delivering the news in Serbian live with technical support from their Albanian engineer. The words on his tee-shirt read: "Radio by young people for young people". June 2001. *Photo by Hélène Caux*

Kael Alford

Kael Alford has been based in Bulgaria since 1996 where she works as a documentary photographer. She has worked throughout the Balkans for American and European publications, including *The Christian Science Monitor, The Houston Chronicle, Die Zeit, NRC Handelsblad* and *The Daily Telegraph*. Alford graduated in journalism from the University of Missouri in the USA and taught photo-journalism at the American University in Bulgaria. Her work includes an ongoing project on the Muslim minority in Bulgaria, as well as extensive coverage of the ethnic communities in Kosovo. She has been with *Liaison / Getty* photo agency since 1999.

Hélène Caux

Hélène Caux began working for UNHCR in Kosovo in July 1999, where she regularly photographed the activities of the agency. UNHCR later commissioned her to publish a photo book on Kosovo. Prior to this assignment she freelanced for various organisations in West Africa and Asia mainly photographing women's and children's issues, such as teenage pregnancy in Mali and street children in Cambodia. Caux also photographed displaced persons and refugees in Croatia in 1997. She has previously worked as a journalist in New York and Paris. Her work appeared in various UN publications, as well as in *New Scientist* and *International Herald Tribune*.

Radhika Chalasani

Radhika Chalasani started her photographic career with *Agence France Press* in Hong Kong in 1990. She then moved to Kenya where she covered the return of Rwandan refugees from the Democratic Republic of Congo, as well as the start of the civil war in 1996 there. Two years later, Chalasani photographed the famine in southern Sudan, a report for which she won an award at the Festival International du Scoop et du Journalisme in Angers, France. In 1997 she received three awards at the Pictures of the Year competition in the USA. Her work has appeared in major magazines including *Time*. She is a regular contributor to UNHCR archives and the *Sipa Press* agency.

Barron Rachman

Barron Rachman first picked up a camera after seeing a picture by Hungarian photographer André Kertész of two children kissing in a refugee camp. From 1990 to 1992, he worked in Paris as an assistant photographer. Rachman then freelanced for the *Philadelphia Enquirer* and the *Associated Press*, and undertook independent assignments in Bosnia-Herzegovina, Israel, Afghanistan, Albania and FYR Macedonia. His work on the exodus and return of Kosovo refugees has appeared in the publications of the *Soros Foundation*. Barron Rachman is presently a freelance photographer and printer in New York.

Hazir Reka

Hazir Reka began to work as a photographer for the Kosovar student magazine *Bota e Re* in 1984, before joining the magazine *Zëri* two years later. His work soon appeared in other newspapers and magazines in the former Yugoslavia, as well as in international publications such as the *New York Times, International Herald Tribune* and *Libération*. He recently published a photo essay on Kosovo titled *Walking in Darkness*, while contributing to other photo books on the region. Reka has exhibited his work in Croatia, Switzerland, France, Saudi Arabia, Spain and Great Britain. He has been a photographer with *Reuters* news agency since 1998.

Andrew Testa

Andrew Testa has been based in the Balkans since 1998. He covered the conflict in Kosovo for *The Observer, The Guardian*, and *Stern* magazine, and has since been photographing news and events in the region for the *New York Times*. Negatives of the pictures he took during the Kosovo war were confiscated by Yugoslav authorities. Luckily, some of the images had been saved digitally and are now displayed in this book. Testa won the Amnesty International Award for Photojournalism in 1999 and has previously won awards in the World Press Photo Competition, the Nikon Press Awards, and the One World Media Awards. His work has also appeared in *Time, Newsweek, Das Magazin, Le Figaro, Die Zeit, Le Monde, Paris Match, Geo* and *Der Spiegel*.

Acronyms

DRC: Danish Refugee Council

EU: European Union

FRY: Federal Republic of Yugoslavia

FYR Macedonia: Former Yugoslav Republic of Macedonia

HEP: Humanitarian Evacuation Programme

ICRC: International Committee of the Red Cross

ICTY: International Criminal Tribunal for the former Yugoslavia

IDPs: Internally Displaced Persons

ICS: Italian Consortium for Solidarity

KFOR: Kosovo Force (NATO-led peacekeeping force in Kosovo)

KLA: Kosovo Liberation Army (UÇK, Ushtria Çlirimtare e Kosovës in Albanian)

KWI: Kosovo Women's Initiative

NATO: North Atlantic Treaty Organisation

NGO: Non-Governmental Organisation

NLA: National Liberation Army (UÇK, Ushtria Çlirimtare Kombëtare in Albanian), armed Albanian group operating in FYR Macedonia

OSCE: Organisation for Security and Co-operation in Europe

UÇPMB: Ushtria Çlirimtare e Preshevës, Medvexhës dhe Bujanocit, armed Albanian group operating in South Serbia in 2000-2001

UN: United Nations

UNHCR: United Nations High Commissioner for Refugees

UNICEF: United Nations Children's Fund

UNMIK: United Nations Interim Administration Mission in Kosovo

WFP: World Food Programme

A Chronology

The photographs in this collection were taken after 1998 to document the role of UNHCR in providing humanitarian support to the displaced, refugee and returnee populations of Kosovo. This chronology is written to help provide context to this work and is not intended to be exhaustive or representative of a broader history.

November 1992: UNHCR opens an office in Prishtinë / Priština, the capital of Kosovo. Initially, work is directed at providing support to 3,000 ethnic Serb refugees from Bosnia-Herzegovina and in later years to some 17,000 Serb refugees from Croatia.

Mid-1990s: Local humanitarian organisations provide support to the increasingly vulnerable Albanian population who, as a result of the revocation of Kosovo's autonomous status by the Milošević regime in 1989, face discrimination and exclusion from public and social services, education and employment. Ibrahim Rugova leads the Kosovo Albanian passive resistance movement.

February - March 1998: Fighting intensifies between Yugoslav forces and the emergent Kosovo Liberation Army after years of rising tensions and human rights abuses by the Yugoslav regime.

A turning point occurs on February 28 when firefights break out between Serb police and the KLA in the villages of Likoshan / Likošane and Çirez / Cirez, where twenty-six Albanians are killed including civilians. On March 5, Yugoslav forces massacre fifty-eight members of the Jashari family in Prekaz I Poshtëm / Donje Prekaze in the Drenica region. Adem Jashari, a founding member of the KLA, is killed during the three days of the fighting. Victims include elderly people, women and children.

May 1998: As fighting continues, UNHCR and international NGOs begin organising regular relief convoys throughout Kosovo for internally displaced persons and for those trapped in their villages.

September 1998: Fourteen Serb policemen are killed during fighting with the KLA near Abri e Epërme / Gornje Obrinje, in Drenica. Special Serb Police forces retaliate against Albanian civilians.

In villages and towns in many parts of Kosovo, unarmed civilians are increasingly coming under attacks and subject to worsening human right abuses. By September, 350,000 Albanians have fled their homes, most of them becoming displaced within Kosovo.

October 27, 1998: Under intense pressure from NATO, President Slobodan Milošević agrees to a cease-fire and partial pull out of Yugoslav forces from Kosovo. The OSCE sends two thousand international monitors to verify the agreement.

January 16, 1999: Forty-five Albanians are found murdered in the village of Reçak / Račak. William Walker, the Chief of the OSCE Kosovo Verification Mission (KVM), publicly refers to crimes against humanity.

February 1999: Talks on substantial autonomy for Kosovo are held in Rambouillet, France, but discussions break down. Tensions rise, and reprisals and abuses worsen against Albanian civilians.

March 23, 1999: The day before NATO airstrikes begin, UNHCR has to halt its humanitarian operations in Kosovo. The agency evacuates its staff following the withdrawal of all other international organisations.

March 24, 1999: NATO launches a seventy-eight-day air offensive against Yugoslav forces in Kosovo, Serbia and Montenegro. Thousands of Albanians from Kosovo begin to arrive in neighbouring Albania and FYR Macedonia on foot, by car and by tractor-trailers.

April 2, 1999: In the single largest twenty-four-hour exodus of the war, an estimated 45,000 people flee from Kosovo and take refuge in FYR Macedonia.

April-May 1999: International agencies and a special NATO humanitarian task force begin to construct camps for refugees in anticipation that they will spend many months in exile. At least 850,000 people, the vast majority of them ethnic Albanians, flee or are expelled from Kosovo, including approximately 445,000 to Albania, 245,000 to Macedonia, and 70,000 to Montenegro. Many are taken in and cared for by host families, while others are cared for in camps overseen by UNHCR. Nearly 100,000 refugees are airlifted from FYR Macedonia to twenty-nine countries as part of the Humanitarian Evacuation Programme.

June 3, 1999: Belgrade accepts a peace plan requiring the withdrawal of all Yugoslav forces from Kosovo and the entry of peacekeepers under a UN mandate.

June 10, 1999: The UN Security Council adopts resolution 1244, setting up the UN Interim Administration Mission in Kosovo (UNMIK). The UNHCR Special Envoy is appointed Humanitarian co-ordinator. With this mandate, UNHCR is given the lead in overseeing the activities of the international humanitarian agencies.

June 12, 1999: NATO and Russian peacekeeping forces enter Kosovo, followed the next day by the first convoy of international humanitarian agencies, led by UNHCR.

June - September 1999: Within three weeks of the signing of the peace accord, more than 600,000 refugees move back into Kosovo in one of the fastest refugee returns in modern history. UNHCR opens offices in seven locations and starts to co-ordinate the humanitarian effort to provide returnees with emergency aid. The agency begins to distribute emergency shelter materials and sets up collective centres for the most vulnerable, as 120,000 houses have been destroyed or are too badly damaged to be reconstructed before winter.

As Kosovo Albanians return en masse, an estimated 150,000 Serbs and Roma flee Kosovo within a period of a few months, seeking safety from Albanian reprisals in Serbia, Montenegro and FYR Macedonia. Displacement of non-Albanians continues during 1999 and 2000, and UNHCR and OSCE further document acts of retaliatory violence against ethnic minorities in Kosovo. Official UNHCR registration of IDPs from Kosovo in Serbia and Montenegro later identify over 230,000 persons displaced since the end of the war.

The vast majority of Kosovo's minority population live in enclaves protected by KFOR. The town of Mitrovica / Mitrovicë is divided in two, with the Serb communities of the northern municipalities rejecting the authority of UNMIK. Most Albanians from the north are forced from their homes and flee to the southern section of Mitrovicë / Mitrovica, while those who stay live under international military protection. At the same time, Serbs and other non-Albanians from the south flee to the north, while those remaining in the south also live under the protection of KFOR.

July 1999: Kosovo Women's Initiative (KWI) is established by UNHCR with funding from the United States' Bureau of Population, Refugees and Migration. It aims at helping Kosovar women and girls rebuild their lives, through projects promoting income generation, education, psycho-social support, reproductive health and legal rights.

Over 1,350 internally displaced Roma and Ashkaelia find safety within a temporary camp, set up by UNHCR and its NGO partners in Kruševac / Krushec. The camp is protected by KFOR.

July 23, 1999: Fourteen ethnic Serb farmers are shot dead as they work in their fields near the village of Staro Gracko / Gracke e Vjetër, in the municipality of Lipjan / Lipljan.

August 1999: UNHCR and the Norwegian Refugee Council establish Legal Aid and Information Centres to give free legal support to the population of Kosovo in areas including property rights, travel documents, humanitarian assistance and family reunification.

September 20, 1999: Some 900 men, women and children leave the Roma / Ashkaelia camp in Kruševac / Krushec and start walking towards the FYR Macedonia border claiming that they have no future in Kosovo. After spending one week camped at the border in precarious conditions, half of them return to the camp in Kosovo while the others are allowed entry to the Stenkovec II camp in FYR Macedonia.

September 1999: Following a grenade attack in Fushë Kosovë / Kosovo Polje, which leaves several Serbs dead and 35 injured, Kosovo leaders, including Albanians, issue condemnations calling for a stop to "cowardly acts of violence against civilians."

October 1999: UNHCR deploys Winter Emergency Teams to distribute food and other aid to the most vulnerable people, especially those in the remote mountain areas of Kosovo.

UNHCR and the Danish Refugee Council establish bus services to assist minorities, mainly Serbs, with improved freedom of movement beyond the confines of enclaves.

October 27, 1999: A UNHCR convoy transporting Serb civilians to Montenegro is attacked by a crowd of over 1,500 people while passing through Peć / Pejë. Fifteen passengers are injured.

November 3, 1999: UNHCR and OSCE release a report on the situation of minorities in Kosovo, documenting widespread violence against ethnic minorities and attacks on their property. UNHCR / OSCE minorities reports are regularly released during the following two years.

November 29, 1999: A Serb man is shot dead and his wife and mother-in-law are savagely assaulted on a crowded street in Prishtinë / Priština amidst celebrations for Albanian Flag Day.

December 6, 1999: OSCE releases a two-volume report covering the period from October 1998 to October 1999. The report provides a grim account of deliberate and massive human rights abuses carried out by Yugoslav forces against Albanians before and during the NATO airstrikes. Among the worst abuses documented are massacres, deliberate killing of civilians including children and the elderly, rapes, forced expulsions, the complete destruction of villages and other war crimes. Later estimates by authorities including the US State Department approximate the number of people killed during this one-year period at ten thousand. These are predominantly people of Albanian ethnicity. The report also documents revenge attacks against ethnic minority civilians by Albanians before, during and after the entry of KFOR.

February - March 2000: Thousands of Albanians from Southern Serbia cross into Kosovo after clashes between Serb forces and the UÇPMB, an armed Albanian group operating in the region. They join some 5,000 Albanians already displaced internally within Kosovo since 1999. Many Albanians left their homes in Southern Serbia when Yugoslav troops, who were forced to withdraw from Kosovo, re-deployed in their villages after June 1999.

February 2, 2000: A UNHCR bus is attacked by a rocket-propelled grenade between Mitrovica / Mitrovicë and Banja / Banjë. Two elderly Serb passengers die and three others are injured. The incident prompts a wave of attacks on Albanians, Muslim Slavs and Turks in the northern part of Mitrovica / Mitrovicë, where Serbs are the majority. On the night of February 3, eight Kosovo Albanians are killed. In the days following, escalating ethnic violence prompts an exodus of some 1,500 non-Serbs, mainly Albanians. Minorities are expelled or flee to the south in fear. Remaining minority families find themselves confined to their homes.

April 12, 2000: UNHCR facilitates the first public meeting since the end of the Kosovo war, between Albanian leaders and Roma-Ashkaelia-Egyptian representatives. They adopt a joint declaration to condemn violence and support rights of the Roma-Ashkaelia-Egyptians in Kosovo, including the right of return.

September – October 2000: Federal elections in the Federal Republic of Yugoslavia (FRY) on September 24 and mass popular protests in the streets of Belgrade that follow remove Slobodan Milošević from power and bring in a new president, Vojislav Koštunica.

October 28, 2000: Municipal elections, organised and monitored by OSCE, are conducted peacefully throughout Kosovo. While most Serbs choose not to participate, the turnout of the Albanian majority reaches 80%. The Democratic League of Kosovo (LDK) led by Ibrahim Rugova captures 58% of the votes.

November 2000: ICTY completes exhumation activities in Kosovo, uncovering 3,623 bodies from 520 grave sites. The majority of the victims are ethnic Albanians. Later in 2001, exhumations in Serbia uncover hundreds of bodies of Albanians murdered in Kosovo during the war in 1999.

November 2, 2000: Despite assurances from Albanian community leaders and preparations by UNHCR to ensure the success of their home coming, four Ashkaelia are brutally executed by unknown perpetrators only forty-eight hours after returning to their village in Dashec / Doševac, Skenderaj / Srbica municipality.

November - December 2000: Renewed fighting in the Preševo / Preshevë valley in southern Serbia between members of the UÇPMB and Serb forces leads to a new influx of 5,000 Albanians into Kosovo.

December 2000: By the end of the year, some 100,000 ethnic Albanians have returned to Kosovo from third countries, including most of those evacuated under HEP. Although the vast majority come back voluntarily, over 12,000 have been forcibly returned. Voluntary and forced returns of ethnic Albanians from third countries continue during 2001.

January 13, 2001: The Joint Committee on Serb Return, comprised of international agencies and Serb representatives, adopts a document affirming the right of Serbs to return to Kosovo and committing to address the conditions preventing return.

February - June 2001: UNHCR reports the arrival in Kosovo of more than 80,000 Albanians mostly from the northern and western regions of FYR Macedonia, fleeing fighting between Macedonian forces and the NLA, an armed Albanian group. The international community and local Albanian families in Kosovo provide assistance to displaced populations as a result of conflict in the region.

February 16, 2001: Eleven Serbs are killed and forty-three injured in a bomb attack on a KFOR-escorted bus convoy near Podujevë / Podujevo. The attack is denounced by the international community and by key Albanian leaders. This attack marks the highpoint of an especially violent three-month period in Kosovo.

April 2001: UNHCR and OSCE release the seventh in a series of reports on the situation of minorities, detailing the unabated ethnically-motivated violence and lack of progress in stabilising the daily situation for Kosovo's ethnic minority communities.

May 2001: The final phase of the hand over of the Ground Safety Zone to FRY authorities is completed. Some of the Albanians from Southern Serbia, who had fled to Kosovo in the previous months, start returning to their homes.

August 2001: Following negotiations by international envoys, representatives of the NLA sign a peace agreement with the FYR Macedonia authorities. They agree to give up their weapons in return for improved status of the Albanian minrity. Refugees hosted in Kosovo begin to return home to FYR Macedonia, and only 10,000 remain in Kosovo by the end of 2001.

August – October 2001: A group of Serbs IDPs begin to return to the Osojane / Osojan valley, where they lived before the war. With the help of international organisations, they start to rebuild their houses, which were mostly destroyed in the aftermarth of the NATO campaign. During the summer and autumn period, several other small-scale organised returns of non-Albanians take place, including a group of Ashkaelia to their homes in urban Prishtinë / Priština. In Kamenicë / Kamenica and Gjilan / Gnjilane municipalities, small groups of Serb and Albanian IDPs co-operate to return and reconstruct their homes in mixed or neighbouring villages.

November 17, 2001: Kosovo wide elections are peacefully conducted, with the participation of all ethnic communities, to elect the Assembly of Kosovo mandated to establish provisional institutions for self-government.

Names in Albanian of villages and cities in Kosovo

Serbia

Monte-
negro

FYR Macedonia

Albania

Novi Pazar
Leposaviq

Zubin Potok
Trepçë
Merdare
Merdar
Zvečan
Podujevë
Suhodoll i Epërme
MITROVICË
Medvedje
Rožaj
Vushtrri
Bajë
Sudenicë
Prekaz i Epërm
Istog
Prekaz i Poshtëm
Skenderaj
Çirez
Plemetin
Osojan
Polac i Ri
Dashec
Likoshan
Obiliq
Graboc i Epërm
Krushec
PRISHTINË
PEJË
Leshtar
Gorazhdec
Klinë
Abri e Epërme
Gllogoc
Fushë Kosovë
Novobërdë
Graçanicë
Kamenicë
Dollc
Llapushnik
Janjevë
Deçan
Medvec
Lipjan
Sllovi
Makresh i Epërm
Vranje
Prejlep
Grackë e Vjetër
Junik
GJILAN
Malishevë
Bujanovac
Rahovec
Reçak
Shtime
GJAKOVË
Samadrexhë
Suharekë
FERIZAJ
Mamushë
Viti
Letnicë
Preševo
Krushë e Vogël
Kovaçec
Kaçanik
Shtërpc
Bob
PRIZREN
Gajrë
Blace
Kumanovo
Moiinë
Stenkovec II
Kukës
Dragash
Neprošteno
Raduša
Stenkovec I
Tetovo
SKOPJE
Čegrane

Kilometers

10   0   10   20

Scale: 1:700,000

The boundaries and names diplayed on this map
do not imply official recognition by the United Nations

	International Border
	Kosovo Boundary
•	Settlement
⋏	Refugee Camps in 1999
	Main Road
	Water Body

PEJË

Elevation with Hillshade, every 500 m

Names in Serbian of villages and cities in Kosovo

Serbia

Monte-negro

FYR Macedonia

Albania

Novi Pazar

Leposavić

Trepča

Podujevo

Merdare

Medvedje

Zvečan

Zubin Potok

Suvi Do   MITROVICA

Vučitrn

Rožaj

Banja

Studenica   ISTOK

Donje Prekaze

Srbica

Cirez

Plemetina

Osojane

Novo Poljance

Likošane

Obilić

 Lještar

Doševac

PRIŠTINA

Gornji Grabovac

Kruševac

Novo Brdo

PEĆ

Gornje Obrinje

Klina

Glogovac

Kosovo Polje

Gračanica

Kamenica

Goraždevac

Dolac

Lapušnik

Janjevo

Dečani

Medvece

Lipljan

Gornji Makreš

Vranje

Prilep

Slovinje

Junik

Staro Gracko

Bujanovac

Mališevo

Štimlje

GNJILANE

Orahovac

Račak

DJAKOVICA

Samodraža

UROŠEVAC

Suva Reka

Mamuša

Vitina

Letnica

Preševo

Mala Kruša

Štrpce

Kovačevac

PRIZREN

Bob   Kačanik

Gajre

Morine

Blace

Kumanovo

kukës

Dragaš

Neprošteno

Raduša

Stenkovec II

Stenkovec I

Čegrane

Tetovo

SKOPJE

Kilometers

10   0   10   20

Scale: 1:700,000

The boundaries and names diplayed on this map
do not imply official recognition by the United Nations

— · — · —	International Border
———	Kosovo Boundary
•	Settlement
▲	Refugee Camps in 1999
———	Main Road
▓▓▓	Water Body

PEJE

Gori

Deçar

Elevation with Hillshade, every 500 m

Designed and printed by Skenpoint,
III Makedonska Brigada, 1000 Skopje,
former Yugoslav Republic of Macedonia.